DonaldShaw.org

PRESENTS...

© 2018 Donald Shaw

Visit the author's website at **www.DonaldShaw.org**

All rights reserved. No portion of this book may be reproduced in any form without permission from the publisher, except as permitted by U.S. copyright law. For permissions contact: info@donaldshaw.org

ISBN: 9781723736766

Disclaimer! The content provided herein is the product of the author's imagination. Therefore, it should be used for entertainment purposes only. Don't try these silly scenarios in real life.

TABLE OF CONTENTS

TABLE OF CONTENTS 3

LET'S START! 4

BONUS: FREE BOOK OF JOKES FOR KIDS 99

REVIEWS AND THE AUTHOR'S PAGE 100

LET'S START!

Would You Rather:

…sleep in a bed for one night with one hundred spiders

become a mosquito for one night?

_____ _____

Would You Rather:

…have a bottomless box of M&M's

– or –

have an always refilling bottle of your favorite juice?

Would You Rather:

…always drink from a saucer

– or –

always eat with your bare hands without a fork or a spoon?

Would You Rather:

…turn invisible whenever you want

– or –

become a five-story-tall giant whenever you feel like?

Would You Rather:

…wash your clothes without a washing machine for a year

– or –

stare at a washing machine in operation for an entire day?

Would You Rather:

…get trapped in the Sahara Desert with one bottle of water

– or –

be left alone on a mountaintop with one small loaf of bread?

Would You Rather:

...have a skateboard as the only means of transportation in your life

have a donkey as the only means of transportation in your life?

Would You Rather:

…laugh uncontrollably every time you hear *"how are you"*

− or −

have your eyes start watering every time you hear the word *"thanks"*?

Would You Rather:

…have a new crayon every time you touch your left ear with your right toe

− or −

have a new balloon every time you lick the tip of your nose?

Would You Rather:

…be a boy who is required to wear a wedding dress on weekends

- or -

be a girl who is required to wear a fake moustache and beard at school?

Would You Rather:

...be forced to read the evening news as loud as you can from 6 to 7pm every day

— or —

be forced to sing Selena Gomez, Lady Gaga, and Justin Bieber songs as loud as you can from 6 to 7am every day?

Would You Rather:

...get a $100,000 gift certificate for a drugstore

– or –

win $1,000 in a lottery?

———  ———

Would You Rather:

…volunteer to clean toilets in an assisted-care facility

– or –

have a wild skunk living in your bathroom for a month?

———  ———

Would You Rather:

…be able to make fantastic animal ice carvings loved by everyone

– or –

create weird paintings, which only a few people understand?

Would You Rather:

…be unable to move your body when you hear the sound of a coffee machine

– or –

be unable to stop running when you hear a dog barking?

Would You Rather:

...sleepwalk every night and wake up in odd places like a supermarket or a library

— or —

only be able to fall asleep on a kitchen table?

Would You Rather:

…lure all pigeons to you whenever they see you

– or –

lure all mosquitos to you whenever they hear you speak?

Would You Rather:

…everyone be required to wear a red thong outside of their pants

– or –

all women and men be required to wear pink skirts at all times, even when they sleep and shower?

___  ___

Would You Rather:

…have to live in a desert with Bedouins for an entire summer

— or —

live in an igloo with Eskimos for an entire polar night?

___  ___

The polar night lasts for more than 24 hours and up to 179 days at the Poles.

Would You Rather:

…play chess boxing – a hybrid of chess and boxing

– or –

take part in a giant pumpkin kayaking race around a lake in hollowed out 800-pound pumpkins?

Would You Rather:

…invent a 3D printer for making ice cream out of water

— or —

teach the world how to make fresh water out of air?

…live in a world without electricity

— or —

in a world where computers and robots control people?

Would You Rather:

…dive into a pool of freezing water to grab a magic ring on its bottom that will fulfil all your wishes

have to run into a burning house to save Aladdin's Lamp?

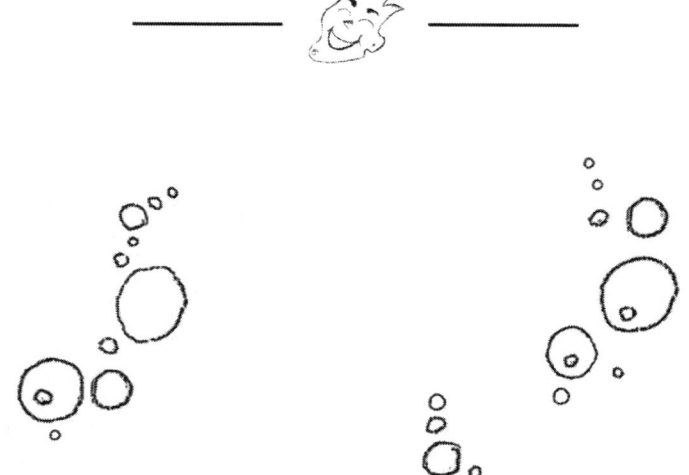

Would You Rather:

…have the FBI hunting you for wearing an alien mask on Halloween

– or –

have the FBI hunting a real alien who happens to be your best friend?

Would You Rather:

...get a job as a professional elephant dresser in Sri Lanka

– or –

become an ear cleaner for people in India?

(both professions actually exist)

Would You Rather:

…live in a world without cars and airplanes

– or –

live in a world without telephones and the Internet?

Would You Rather:

…have absolutely no hair

– or –

have lots of hair all over your body?

Would You Rather:

…be very rich but have no talents

– or –

be the most gifted person in the world but have no money?

Would You Rather:

…be required to paint your nails every hour

– or –

have to color your eyebrows the colors of the rainbow every day?

Would You Rather:

…have terrible dandruff that can't be treated

have horrible body odor that can't be washed off?

Would You Rather:

…be the worst horse rider in history and wind up broke and alone

– or –

be the best riding horse in the world and live like a millionaire but in the body of the horse?

Would You Rather:

…be so afraid of the sun you'd have to relocate to the world's rainiest village in India

– or –

be so afraid of the rain you'd have to relocate to Death Valley, which averages just about 2 inches of rain in an entire year?

Would You Rather:

…eat a large bowl of fried cockroaches for your next lunch

– or –

starve without any food or water for three whole days?

Would You Rather:

…have a $1 coin fall down near you from nowhere every time you sneeze

— or —

have a $1 bill appear in your pocket from nowhere every time you call a random unknown person *"Your Majesty"*?

Would You Rather:

…always look like you are 100 years old but live for 300 years

— or —

always look like you're 20 years old but only live for 70 years?

Would You Rather:

…have to build a tree house to survive in the jungle

– or –

have to occupy a wild bear's cave to survive on a mountain?

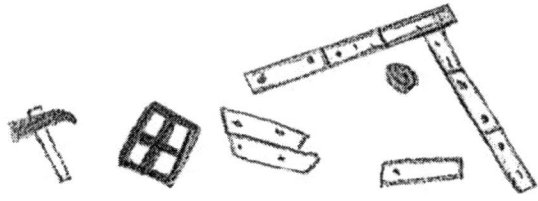

Would You Rather:

…always have free WI-FI and unlimited battery power on all your devices

— or —

have unlimited free food and drink for you and your friends every time you go to any restaurant?

Would You Rather:

…have everything you draw become real

— or —

have everything you say become a law?

Would You Rather:

…be able to fly as fast as you can walk

— or —

be able to run as fast as a helicopter can fly?

Would You Rather:

…have zebra-style stripes all over your body

— or —

replace your right hand with the one of a giant crab?

___  ___

Would You Rather:

…get an email from a stranger that always gives you the answer to any question you ever have

– or –

get a parcel with a magic stick inside that can fulfill your three wishes?

Would You Rather:

…find yourself on an inhabited tropical island without any tools, clothes, or shelter

— or —

find yourself on an uninhabited arctic island with an unlimited supply of food, water, and clothes, and a safe and warm house in which to live?

Would You Rather:

…have a luxury apartment in any city of the world with a restriction never to leave that city

have an average apartment in all the world's capital cities but be required to relocate to a different city every month?

Would You Rather:

…invent a machine that can turn stones into cookies

− or −

create a refrigerator that can quickly grow fruits and vegetables inside?

Would You Rather:

…know every fact from Wikipedia and have the highest IQ in history

– or –

have below average intelligence but be able to make each of your friends happy?

Would You Rather:

…have unbearable neighbors who party every night till the morning, break glass, scream, but never come to your apartment

— or —

have very sweet and quite neighbors who have the key to your apartment and come to visit you several times a day, even when you are asleep or not at home?

Would You Rather:

…have to use a parachute to save your life in a burning airplane

— or —

have to go over Niagara Falls in a barrel to save yourself from hungry cannibals?

Would You Rather:

…be twice as strong when you have a live insect in your mouth

– or –

run backwards as fast as a sports car when you have a live mouse in your palm?

Would You Rather:

…swap bodies with the ugliest person in the world

– or –

swap bodies with the world's cutest dog?

————  ————

Would You Rather:

…always have your favorite food for breakfast but be forced to eat it in cattle shed

– or –

always have your least favorite food for lunch but be able to choose any place in the world where you can eat it?

Would You Rather:

…wake up on the Moon with clear directions on how to get back to Earth

wake up in the middle of an unknown desert with a helicopter but without instructions on how to use it?

Would You Rather:

…have to watch your favorite movie every day

— or —

never be able to watch any movie, TV show, or YouTube video for the rest of your life?

Would You Rather:

…have each person you ask for a ride be ready to give you one

— or —

have each person you meet be ready to buy you a new T-shirt?

Would You Rather:

…touch a vacuum cleaner dust bag with your tongue once a day

become super allergic to ice cream?

Would You Rather:

…have to clean your room which is filled with broken bottles

– or –

have to clean your room which has ten little mice under your bed?

Would You Rather:

…eat a hamburger with maple syrup

– or –

eat a jelly pizza with peanut butter?

Would You Rather:

…have your toilet clog every Monday morning

– or –

have no tap water every Tuesday evening?

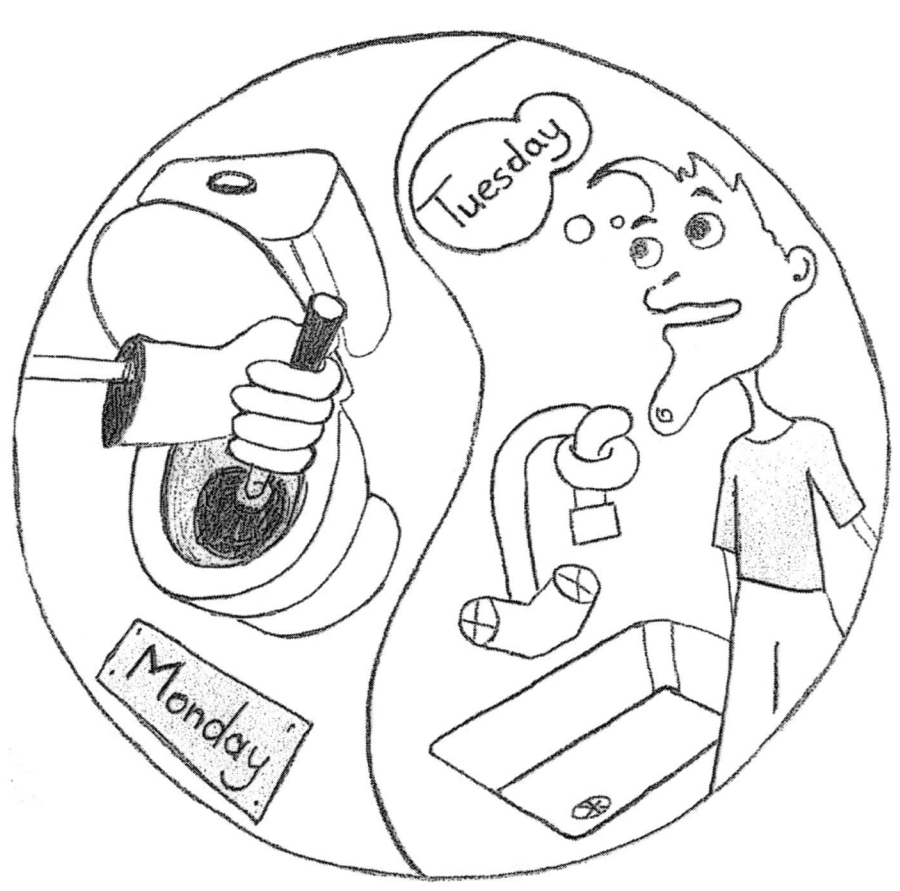

Would You Rather:

…live in a world where the most popular sounds are chainsaw, a fire-engines' siren, and a leaf blower played 24/7 on radio, TV, and used by most people as ringtones

– or –

live in a world where any type of music is prohibited?

Would You Rather:

…beg for money in an underground walkway

– or –

get paid to wear T-shirts with very stupid ads?

Would You Rather:

…always be awakened at 6am by the sound of an unknown baby crying nearby

– or –

listen to a poorly played violin for 30 minutes every night before you fall asleep?

Would You Rather:

…never see a river, a lake, or an ocean in your whole life

— or —

have to live on a small floating island in the middle of the ocean and eat solely whatever fish you can catch?

Would You Rather:

…write an awesome book for kids, but one that only a few people read

— or —

film a very stupid soap opera which becomes so popular that raving fans and paparazzi won't ever leave you alone?

———

Would You Rather:

…win one million dollars in a giveaway on Instagram but have obligation to spend it for charity

— or —

find $10 in your pocket every morning for the rest of your life?

Would You Rather:

…hide from monsters every Friday the 13th night

– or –

turn into a real vampire every Halloween?

Would You Rather:

…be colorblind

– or –

have a job that requires you to explain the difference between colors to colorblind people?

Would You Rather:

…have pink hair by nature without the ability to change its color

– or –

have naturally green skin?

———      ———

Would You Rather:

…live in a place where the weather changes drastically every ten minutes from winter to summer and back, and from rain to high heat and then to snow

◠ or ◠

live in a place where it's eternally spring but it's ten times easier than usual to get sunburn, so that everyone has to use sunscreen every ten minutes?

Would You Rather:

...spend an hour in a cage with a live tiger

− or −

sit on a chair on the edge of a cliff during a snowstorm?

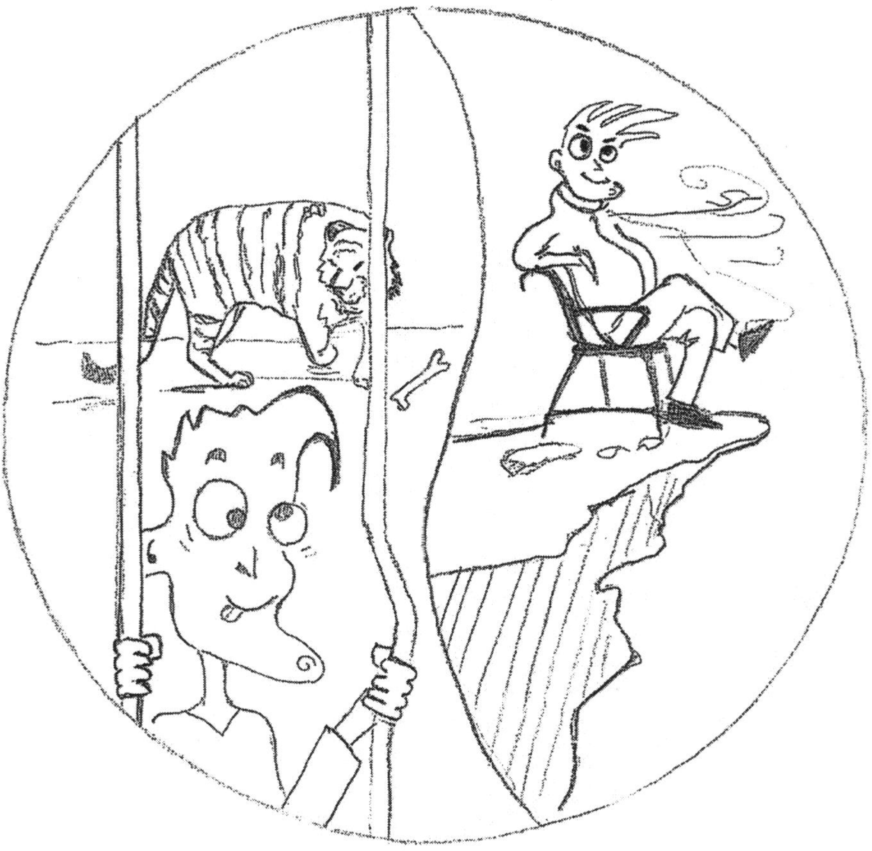

Would You Rather:

…invent a device that provides free Wi-Fi in every corner of the planet

– or –

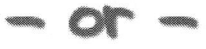

find the way to save the Amur leopard, the world's most endangered cat, from extinction?

Would You Rather:

…discover a way to wipe out all human diseases forever

discover a way to stop wars forever?

Would You Rather:

…become famous for eating the world's largest pizza

— or —

get recognition for bursting balloons with your back faster than anyone else in the world?

Would You Rather:

…live in a parallel world where people have wings, fly like birds, and make nests

— or —

live on a planet where people can walk through walls and understand the animals?

Would You Rather:

…drink a can of Coca Cola every hour you are awake

— or —

never drink soda in your entire life?

Would You Rather:

…be crazy and think you are a medieval king

— or —

be a medieval king's slave in reality?

Would You Rather:

…have the name of your favorite movie star tattooed on your forehead

— or —

have the name of your least favorite singer tattooed on your hand?

Would You Rather:

…be able to blow fire like a dragon

– or –

change the color of your skin like a chameleon?

Would You Rather:

…always have toilet paper finish on you before you have completely cleaned your butt

– or –

always be one minute late for scheduled events, such as the start of movies and meetings and the time for airplane departures?

Would You Rather:

…always have the ugliest haircuts in history

– or –

have to walk barefoot for the rest of your life?

Would You Rather:

…have a belly button on your back

have three rows of eyebrows?

Would You Rather:

…spend a whole week in a Lamborghini without the ability to get out of it

— or —

never be able to own a car?

Would You Rather:

…live in a world where people speak different languages in every city and town

— or —

live in a world where all people are required to wear uniform?

___  ___

Would You Rather:

…drink all your beverages from a tablespoon

eat all your food through a straw?

___  ___

Would You Rather:

…have edible spaghetti hair that regrows once you eat it

— or —

have fingernails made of chocolate?

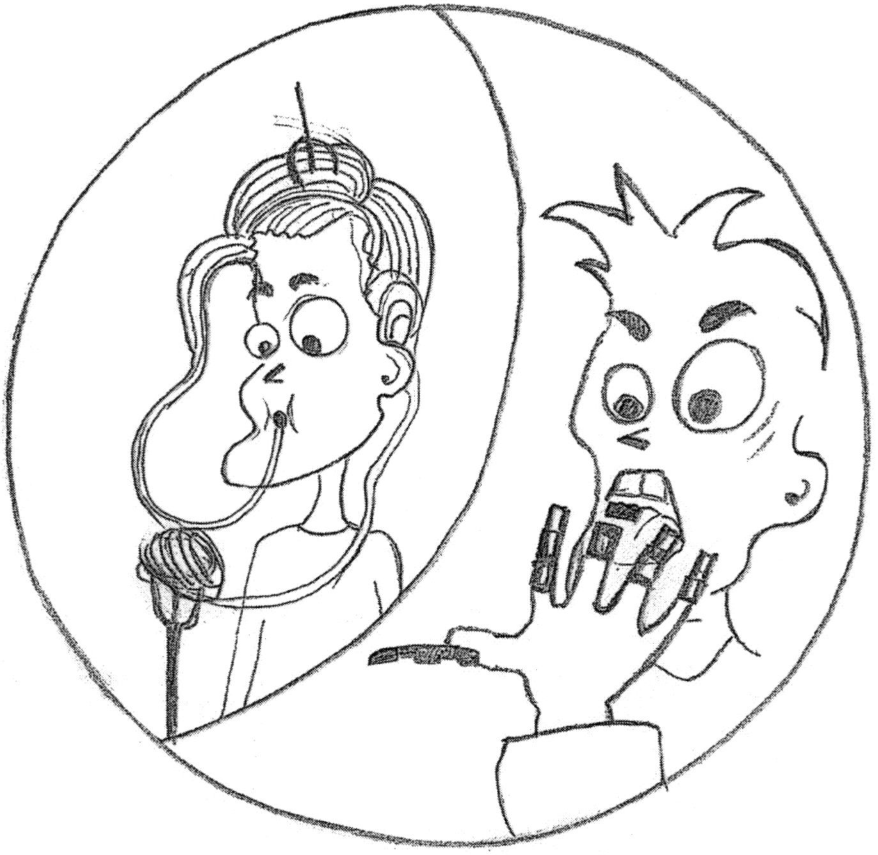

Would You Rather:

…be forever cursed to fall each time you start running

– or –

be living near a beautiful lake all your friends love to swim in, but be cursed to feel like you are drowning every time you try to learn how to swim?

―――― 😄 ――――

Would You Rather:

…completely lose your voice whenever you hear music playing

◠ or ◠

turn into a mermaid for an hour once a week?

Would You Rather:

…replace your nose with the trunk of an elephant

replace your head with the head of a horse?

Would You Rather:

...live in a world where all pandas are yellow and blue

− or −

live in a world where all crocodiles are orange?

Would You Rather:

...draw the logo of your favorite cartoon and get very rich and famous

− or −

make friends with the characters of your favorite cartoon who turn out to be real?

Would You Rather:

...own Burj Khalifa [in Dubai, United Arab Emirates], the tallest building in the world

― or ―

own ten of the world's fastest cars, including a Hennessey Venom F5, Bugatti Chiron, and a Tesla Roadster?

Would You Rather:

…see the face of *Hello Kitty* instead of yours every time you look at the mirror

— or —

see the face of a random *Pokémon* instead of yours every time you look at the mirror?

Would You Rather:

...eat a Happy Meal at McDonald's on Thanksgiving Day

— or —

get a Christmas present you really don't want?

Would You Rather:

...have to deal with rude shop assistants and door-to-door salesmen every time you are in a hurry

– or –

step in dog poo as often as you wear shoes?

Would You Rather:

…be allowed to take a shower just twice in your life

– or –

live in a swimming pool?

Would You Rather:

...wear someone's used underwear every day

— or —

always eat and drink while sitting in the bathroom?

Would You Rather:

...sleep on used diapers instead of a pillow

— or —

pee on yourself in public?

———  ———

Would You Rather:

…press your finger into the school bus driver's nostril

live in a school bus for thirty days?

———  ———

Would You Rather:

…sleep every night in a tent with the world's smelliest man

– or –

stub your toe at least every hour?

Would You Rather:

…have an endless amount of money on your cell phone balance

– or –

have free life-time access to all PlayStation releases?

Would You Rather:

…mumble all the time, so that the others can hardly understand you

— or —

talk very loud all the time, so that others have to put their hands over their ears every time you speak?

Would You Rather:

…have all plants scream when you step over or cut them

hear the voices of every toy that has a mouth?

- THE END -

BONUS: FREE BOOK OF JOKES FOR KIDS

Thanks for reading the book! We hope you had fun!

For a limited time, you can get a funny book pictured here for FREE!

Donald Shaw has given away thousands of hilarious Kindle books for free. If you would like to be one of those who receives his titles when they are free, discounted, or newly released please go to: **http://DonaldShaw.org/gift/**

REVIEWS AND THE AUTHOR'S PAGE

Your reviews are extremely important!

If you enjoyed reading this book, please consider leaving me a short review on the book's Amazon page. That really is the best way you can help new readers find my book. I would really appreciate it!

Check out my profile on Amazon and read humor books for kids and adults. Search for: Donald Shaw. Thank you!

Made in the USA
Middletown, DE
07 December 2018